To: _____

From: _____

Other Books by Gregory E. Lang:

GOOD LUCK, GRADUATE

GRADUATE

223 Thoughts for the Road Ahead

GREGORY E. LANG

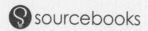

Published by Sourcebooks, Inc.
P.O. Box 4410, Naperville, Illinois 60567–4410
(630) 961–3900
Fax: (630) 961–2168
www.sourcebooks.com

Printed and bound in the United States of America.
LB 10 9 8 7 6 5 4 3 2 1

To Meagan and Linley.
May the legacy you leave be salt
and light for those you love.

GOOD LUCK, GRADUATE

INTRODUCTION

A few years ago, I reflected on the significance of my daughter Meagan reaching her sixteenth birthday. I thought of the milestones she had already achieved in her short lifetime, and of my pride and heart pains, as I knew each milestone she reached brought her closer to coming of age and decreasing her dependence on me. Those years ago, I wanted to impart to her all the reassurances, warnings, and bits of advice I hoped she would consider, not only when alone in the driver's seat, but as she continued to mature into her own person, making plans and decisions without the necessity of sage parental consent.

As most parents do, I realized I still had much to teach my daughter before she set out on her own, and I took every opportunity to help her notice the important life lessons she would encounter. We discussed the perils of misusing a credit card, the wisdom of understanding your health insurance before going to the doctor, and the details of entering into a lease agreement, securing utilities, registering to vote, and much, much more.

The day our family drove away and left Meagan standing alone in the center of her college dorm room, I was confident she was prepared for her independence. That evening, however, when I passed by her empty bedroom, I wondered if I had indeed taught her all she needed to know. I thought too about the youngest in our household, Linley, who then was within a year of receiving her learner's permit, and who was yet to receive all the warnings, teachings, and fear-driven prayers we had given her older step-sister.

It is a worry all parents experience, I suppose, wondering if their children are ready to face the challenges of the future. It is probably also a frustration every child experiences, wishing their parents would worry less and trust more, wishing their parents would have faith in their own parenting skills and believe their child is ready and able to handle what may come. It is a lesson both girls have gone to great lengths to teach me—that while parenting does indeed mean helping your child, it equally means stepping away in the right moments to give the freedom and room for growth. It was difficult knowledge for me to accept, but wisdom I am grateful for today.

As I write this, two milestones, one for each girl, are

fast approaching, even arriving somewhat sooner than expected. Through their own determined efforts, Linley is graduating high school a year early and is eager to leave home to attend college, and Meagan is finishing college early, eager to graduate school and begin her career. So once again, I reflect on the significance of children graduating and going solo…

…and I put my concerns aside, having faith in our prayers and our teachings, and in the girls' own natural resources and abilities. I smile at their bold confidence and assured willfulness, marvel at their expanding, brilliant minds, take pride in their growing list of achievements, and stand amazed at how each in her own way has surpassed my hopes and dreams of how she would turn out.

And yet, I remain a parent with the impulse to make sure my children are safe, happy, and destined to prosper. So even though, given the chance, they might have convinced me it was an unnecessary exercise, I penned this book. I wrote it to capture just one more round of fatherly advice and simple suggestions for living a fulfilled life, and I wrote it as a remedy for when they might be perplexed, in need of a reassuring voice, and far away from home. And I wrote this book to remind them of the love their parents have for them.

Yes, I remain a parent, no matter how old and how accomplished the girls might be. And as a parent, I will also—always, I'm sure—remain proud of what they do and who they become in their journeys. I can't wait to watch them get there.

But what about you?

This book is in your hands because someone, likely a loving parent or two, maybe a mentor or grandparent, is proud of the moment to which you have arrived—your graduation. Be it from high school, undergraduate college, vocational or professional school, or whatever the case, you have met the challenge, you have passed the test, you have proven your worthiness and ability and shown your potential, and you are about to enter a new stage in your life, a stage where you can bring to bear the benefits of what you have learned thus far.

Before you is a free and diverse world, and within it a waiting opportunity to become a part of something larger than yourself—an opportunity to right wrongs, mend wounds, create something fabulous, or discover something astonishing. No matter what the opportunity may be for you, at its core is the call for you to use your gifts in a way that makes a difference. And I promise you, when you choose to make that difference, be it for one person or a nation, you will have begun to define your good legacy. The time between now and then is your journey, and this book was given to you by someone who loves you and wishes to assure that you travel safely. Do, and remember to call home now and then.

1.   Pay attention to where you are going.
     If you see that you're headed in the
     wrong direction, turn around
     before you go too far.

2.   When you are tired, take a break.
     And get enough sleep, too.

3.   Buy a camera and use it often.

4. Don't be photographed doing something you wouldn't want to explain later.

5. Be comfortable with yourself. It isn't necessary to be like everyone else.

6. Learn one new thing every day.

7. Always congratulate those who beat you at something. It's good sportsmanship.

8. Don't get bogged down in a swamp of secrets. You may not find your way out easily.

9. Don't stand by as friends wander into danger, but pull them back to safety. You are then a true friend.

10. You can't always rely on your own judgment. Surround yourself with people whose opinions you respect and trust.

11. When there is enough blame to go around, always take your fair share.

12. Always share the spotlight. No one ever accomplished anything good all by themselves.

13. Know what brings out the worst in you and avoid it, but immerse yourself in what brings out your best.

14. Think before you speak. Words cannot be taken back—they linger in memory forever.

15. Believe in miracles. They really do occur.

16. Forgive and forget. There's no point wasting time remembering the wrongs committed against you.

17. Make prayer a daily habit.

18. Don't procrastinate. It keeps you from getting things done.

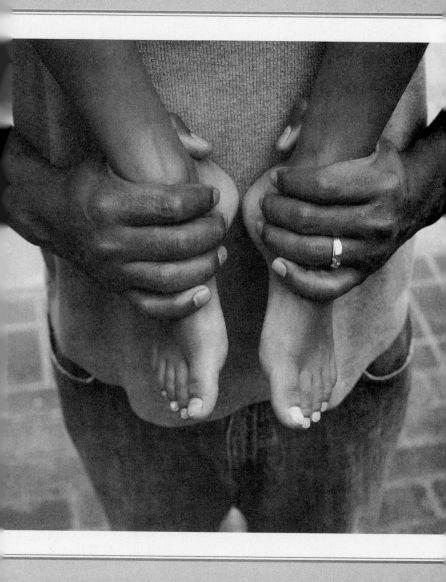

19. Be honest on your resume, and sell yourself during the interview.

20. Before beginning your career, take one wild and crazy job. You'll always be so glad you did.

21. Always use the spell-checker before you send an email.

22. Always wait at least twenty-four hours before sending an email written in anger.

23. All work and no play makes you quite dull. All play and no work makes you flat broke. Balance work and play.

24. Be understanding of your parents' fears as they grapple with letting go of you. It is just another sign of how much they love you.

25. Research trips, careers, and expenses—before you undertake them. It'll save you big headaches later.

26. Make time now for those who love you. You never know how much or how little time you might have to give later.

27. Don't weigh yourself every day. You'll drive yourself crazy.

28. A pet is a lot of fun, but also a lot of responsibility. Don't get one until you are up to a big challenge.

29. If your grandmother wouldn't recognize it, don't eat it.

30. Learn how to play at least one sport. You don't have to be good at it, just able to play it.

31. Pay attention to current events. New world history is made every day, and you're a part of that world.

32. You must take care of things to make them last. That goes for relationships, too.

33. Donate the things you don't use. If you haven't used them in years, someone else certainly can.

34. Be anonymous now and then. It makes your good deeds even better.

35. When invited over for dinner, always bring a little something with you.

36. Remember that price doesn't always equal value or taste. Shop wisely.

37. Don't badmouth others, particularly via email. You never know who is going to forward your message on.

38. If you live in an upstairs apartment, walk softly between 9 p.m. and 6 a.m.

39. If you must talk on the cell phone, go outside. No one wants to know your business.

40. Stretch your limits once in a while. You may find you have more range than you thought.

41. Learn to love yourself before you try to love someone else. Only then can you love another as honestly as you should.

42. Be on time. There is no such thing as "fashionably late," especially at work.

43. Accept the criticism of others.
You will never be perfect,
your efforts never flawless.

44. If you must criticize someone, do so
gently or your words won't be heard.

45. Learn how to set a table and which
utensil to use when. It's impressive.

46. Put things back where you found them, especially those that belong to someone else.

47. Don't relive the mistakes of the past—there are plenty of mistakes to be made in the future.

48. Never pull away from a hug.

49. When you feel like crying, do.

50. Walk away from a fight, even one you could win. That's real strength.

51. Always have a healthy dose of fear. To be fearless is to be just plain foolish.

52. You cannot make someone love you, but you can be someone who can be loved.

53. Never let the words "I told you so" leave your mouth.

54. Avoid wasting water—there are millions who don't have access to it at all.

55. Take care not to ask too much of your friends.

56. War is easy to start but difficult to end. Choose peace.

57. If you are an expert at something, share your knowledge with someone else.

58. Buy cheap sunglasses. It's always the expensive ones that you lose.

59. Work to improve your writing skills. The ability to write a good letter or proposal is a valuable asset.

60. Say what's on your mind, but say it with diplomacy.

61. Don't judge others. It's the diversity of personalities in the world that keeps life interesting!

62. If you wake up on the wrong side of the bed, take care not to ruin the morning for everyone else.

63. Stay calm during a crisis.

64. Don't stand by a bad decision. A changed mind is better than a stubborn one.

65. Be someone who others can lean on in times of need or sorrow. Then, when it's your time to lean, they will be there for you.

66. Don't let success go to your head. It will lead to failure.

67. Maintain a healthy dose of skepticism. It'll save you from a fatal dose of gullibility.

68. Don't always be in charge, but take charge when no one else will.

69. If you have led others to expect something from you, don't get mad when eventually they do.

70. Find a cause you believe in, and donate what you can, when you can.

71. Don't ask for or seek pity.

72. Recognize that not everyone will like you. Don't be bothered by it when someone doesn't.

73. There is a lot to see in this world. Go see it.

74. It's true: You need to see a doctor once a year; a dentist, twice.

75. Remember that speeding rarely gets you anywhere faster.

76. Don't be afraid to give and receive love.

77. Be independent. Running with the pack isn't always the best decision.

78. Loyalty begets loyalty.
Be loyal.

79. Be trustworthy. It is an honor to be trusted.

80. Have mercy, for being without mercy gets you nowhere worth going.

81. Try to be logical, not just emotional.

82. Be nice to strangers. You never know in what setting your paths will cross again.

83. Notwithstanding the above, always regard strangers with a little caution.

84. Learn what "notwithstanding" means; you'll see it more often than you think.

85. No matter what your politics, always be liberal in matters of grace.

86. Never lie. You will get caught, sooner or later, and the truth is so much easier to remember.

87. Stop to take stock of your life now and then. You'll always find yours is better than you might have thought.

88. It's easier to lose someone's respect than it is to earn it. Once it's earned, be sure to keep it.

89. Become skilled in the art of saying "no" firmly and with style.

90. If "no" is the correct response, say it immediately rather than eventually.

91. Whenever you're near the beach, go put your feet in the water.

92. Set goals. Write them down. Pursue them. Reward yourself when you achieve one. Then set a new goal.

93. Never sign a contract you don't understand—especially one relying heavily on the word "notwithstanding."

94. Forgive your parents for their mistakes. They probably meant well at the time.

95. When you're sick, stay home. No one else wants what you have.

96. Read instructions carefully and completely, even if you think you already know what to do.

97. Keep thank-you notes on hand. Use them often—very often.

98. Keep a list of things to do. When you feel bored, pull it out and get busy.

99. Always dress appropriately for the given occasion, remembering it is better to be overdressed than underdressed.

100. Rather than wait for others to come to you, go to them.

101. Learn the art of conversation. Practice it often.

102. Always pay your bills, taxes, and tithes on time.

103. Don't believe everything you read on the Internet.

104. Gossip is like a virus—it spreads fast. Very fast. Don't gossip.

105. A fact of life: Everyone, even you, has hurts, habits, and hang-ups.

106. Clean breaks heal faster. When a relationship is over, let it be over.

107. When friends and loved ones need to vent, let them.

108. Change your PIN and passwords often.

109. When a guest in others' homes, respectfully observe their customs.

110. Eat at least one bite of everything someone has cooked for you.

111. Begin your day with a hearty, healthy breakfast.

112. When your life isn't going according to plan, ask yourself if you have the right plan.

113. It's impossible to be right all the time, so stop believing that *right now*.

114. Be a humble winner and a gracious loser.

115. Dignity isn't nonrenewable. If you lose it, you can get it back.

116. Don't hesitate to say "I don't understand" when you don't.

117. If you said you would, do. If you said you wouldn't, don't.

118. Know your limits. Don't
overindulge in anything.

119. Think twice, even three times, before
getting a tattoo.

120. When you've done something
wrong, don't try to get out of it.
Facing consequences is a part
of life.

121. Be thankful for what you have and waste none of it.

122. Be wary of alcohol, for where drunkenness goes, debauchery follows.

123. Be transparent, not mysterious. When you leave others guessing, you may not like their conclusions.

124. Always park in a well-lit, conspicuous place. Nothing good lurks in the dark.

125. Contribute time and money generously when you can. When you can't, make up for it later.

126. Don't forget to stop and smell the roses—literally. Watch the sun rise, too.

127. Take your—and only your—
medication as directed.

128. Control your temper—or
it will control you.

129. Live by the Golden Rule
every day.

130. Worry more about doing the right things than if you're doing things for the right person. The latter results only in doing the right thing less often.

131. Believe it or not, someone is looking up to you. Be a good example.

132. Always tell the truth and expect the same from others.

133. Reciprocate every act of kindness *and* pay it forward.

134. Understand that every trespass doesn't call for a response. Sometimes it's best simply to do nothing.

135. Be without prejudice; there's no justifiable excuse for it.

136. Give more than you take in every relationship to which you commit yourself.

137. Make a fool of yourself once in a while. Being serious all the time is exhausting.

138. Study days in advance of a test. You will forget too much if you cram at the last minute.

139. Stay in touch with those you love. They'd like to hear from you more often than you think.

140. Feelings are a strength, not a weakness. Embrace and demonstrate your feelings.

141. Don't be totally dependent on repairmen. Learn how to fix some things yourself.

142. Diversify your portfolio, your work experience, and your social circle.

143. This too is true: It is far better to be a gentle servant than a cruel master.

144. Make compound interest work for you. Start saving early. Save a lot.

145. Practice listening with your heart instead of your ears.

146. Hold yourself to the same—or higher—standard to which you hold others.

147. Let sleeping dogs lie, and they won't reach back to bite you.

148. Be scrupulously honest in all dealings, especially those that involve love or money.

149. Self-control isn't all it's cut out to be. Lose control every now and then—it's liberating.

150. Sometimes carelessness follows confidence. Don't get too confident.

151. Never turn your back on your friends and family.

152. Don't ignore your body. If something doesn't seem right, see a doctor.

153. You cannot repent unless you first confess. Confess with an honest heart.

154. Hold yourself accountable to those who love you.

155. Take care with what you post on the Internet. Once it's out there, you lose control of it.

156. Never begin a first date at your home, but rather in a convenient public place.

157.   Always review your check before paying for the meal.

158.   Balance your checkbook each month, to the penny.

159.   Keep a little room in the budget for the unexpected.

160. Become an expert at mending fences. Be the first to say "I'm sorry."

161. Remember that the best advice is that which is asked for.

162. Date only one person at a time. It's less confusing—and cheaper.

163. Always save some time and energy for yourself.

164. Be carefree when you can, but never when you shouldn't.

165. If you spend less money than you have, you will always have a little money left.

166. Keep emergency contact numbers in your wallet, and save them in your phone.

167. When given a chance to walk in someone else's shoes, do it.

168. When in doubt, call your parents for advice.

169. Remember that it is never too late to ask for forgiveness. And it is never too early to give it, either.

170. Always stand during the national anthem. Better yet, sing along, too.

171. Save yourself regret in your old age. Exercise often and eat well, beginning now.

172. Life is much like a road trip. Plan ahead and be safe. Enjoy the journey.

173. Live in the moment to get the most from it. Plan for the future to get the most from it, too.

174. Give praise often. Your encouragement may motivate someone who needs it.

175. Remember that with age comes wisdom. Befriend someone older and learn a thing or two.

176. Be accepting of those who are different from you. They, in turn, will be accepting of you.

177. Always give two weeks' notice when leaving a job, and give your best effort during those two weeks. You'll need the good reference one day.

178. Be a reasonable skeptic,
not an absolute contrarian.

179. Never be the last to leave a party,
unless you plan to lend a hand
cleaning up the mess.

180. Don't be fooled by statistics,
for there is always a margin
of error.

181. It's more important to care about what your loved ones think than what strangers think.

182. Find the best in everyone, no matter how hard you might have to look.

183. Keep a journal. You may not read it for years, but when you do, you'll be glad you wrote things down.

184. Consider this: A volunteer position just might be the most rewarding job you'll ever have.

185. Show up when you are least expected, for that is often when you are most needed.

186. Giving brings you more treasure than you could ever acquire.

187. Don't post a status update you wouldn't want your mother to read.

188. Use virus protection, and I mean in every applicable situation.

189. Ask others to change something about themselves only if you are willing to change something about yourself.

190. There's a big difference between needs and wants. It will serve you well to know the difference.

191. Wear your heart on your sleeve. Love isn't meant to be kept secret.

192. Never give personal identification data to anyone you don't know.

193. Don't put more on a credit card than you can pay for in ninety days.

194. Learn something from what others attempt to teach you. Then teach still others what you have learned.

195. It's better to start something you can't finish than to start something you can't stop.

196. Deal with the ugly stuff first, and save the beautiful stuff for last. It will be even more beautiful by then.

197. Laugh often, and laugh with gusto, even if at yourself. Actually, even more so if at yourself.

198. There will be fender benders in life. Take them all in stride.

199. Look over your shoulder occasionally to see where you have been. Don't forget from where you have come.

200. When someone is in need, extend your hand.

201. Respect personal space—everyone has a right to their own.

202. Don't let a chance to say "thank you" pass you by.

203. Have a compass, so that you always know where you're headed. Have a moral compass, too.

204. When someone ends a presentation with "Any questions?" ask one.

205. Make sure your windows and doors are shut and locked before you go to bed.

206. If you break or lose something you borrow, replace it with something better.

207. Resist the temptation to increase your standard of living with every pay raise.

208. Always follow others at a safe distance. You never know what they may suddenly do.

209. Observe all things in your surroundings, not just what is directly in front of you. It's the things that sneak up on you that frighten you most.

210. Keep a well-stocked first-aid kit near at hand.

211. Pain is a part of life. Learn to tolerate it well.

212. Remember that it's better to call home and ask for a ride than it is to drive when you shouldn't.

213. Avoid comparing your current love to former ones. Let each stand on his or her own.

214. Respect other people's religious beliefs. Engage them in conversation, not debate.

215. Remember to use your turn signals. It's important to let others know your intentions.

216. Love knows no schedule. Be patient. Seize it when it comes along.

217. Smile at everyone. When you do, so many more people will begin smiling at you.

218. Have at least one recipe you can cook for company.

219. Always remember your way home, and be sure to go back there every once in a while.

220. If it seems too good to be true, it most likely is.

221. Make a difference in the world, not for your own rewards, but for the good of many.

222. You can't cross a burned bridge. Take care not to burn bridges, unless you're willing to rebuild them.

223. Leave a legacy that inspires.

ACKNOWLEDGMENTS

In this book about living a good life well, I wish to say thanks to some of those who have given me abundant love, support, direction, and encouragement—Gene and Dianne Lang, Stanley Brown, Eddie Brown, Mary Jean Register, Elaine Brown, Jimmy and Sandra Kennedy, O. L. Brown, John Buhman, Dan Donovan, Al Kramer, Alistair Deakin, Ron Pitkin, Lisa Taylor, Janet Moran, Richard Endsley, Karen Wampler, Jim and Linda Walters, Lee Perdue, Peter Brown, Cindy Zeagler-Stevens, Patricia DeBary, Brandi Leaptrot, Laura Dean, Allison Aden, Keith Compton, Chip Traynor, Kristina Holmes, Stacy Collins, Debra Potter, Jackie Dieter, Chip Sweney, Drue Warner, Johnny and Joann Parris, and my incredible-beyond-my-wildest-dreams wife, Jill Lang.

TO CONTACT THE AUTHOR

Write in care of the publisher:
Gregory E. Lang
c/o Sourcebooks, Inc.
P.O. Box 4410
Naperville, IL 60567-4410

Email the author or visit his website:
gregoryelang@gmail.com
www.gregoryelang.com